KLEYIYA

a book for children

INSPIRED

BY CLÉIA FARGÈRE XININDLU

KLEYIYA

Hello!

my name is Kleyiya

Today's theme is 'Butterfly'.

Come along!

Hello friends!
Let's talk about caterpillars and butterflies

2

Caterpillar

Caterpillar

Butterfly

Turning into a butterfly

Butterfly

Butterflies everywhere !
Oh look at this...
A butterfly lives for
15 – 29 Days.
6

Your turn

Did You Know that...?

You are not always going to be a caterpillar.

You can also transform into a beautiful butterfly one day if you want.

Let's colour

Colour Me In Red and Yellow

KLEYIYA

Let's colour

Let's colour

Colour these Caterpillars

Let's colour

Colour this Butterfly

Let's colour

Colour these Butterflies

Let's colour

Colour this Butterfly

Let's colour

Let's colour

Colour down below

Let's colour

Colour down below

Let's colour

Colour this Butterfly

Complete

Complete this Butterfly

Did You Know?

Butterflies live in oval-shaped foliage and in tree hollows, Oh! they also live in rocks.

Complete

Complete this Butterfly

Did You Know?

A butterfly can have lots of hundreds of eggs

Complete

Complete this Caterpillar

Did You Know?

Caterpillars are members of the order Lepidoptera

Let's Count

How many...?

=_ _ _ _ _ _ butterfly

Let's Count

How many...?

=______ butterflies

Let's Count

=______ butterflies

Let's Count

=_ _ _ _ _ _ caterpillars

Let's Count

=_ _ _ _ _ _ flowers

Shapes

Let's learn...

A flower in a square

Shapes

Let's learn...

A flower in a triangle

Shapes

Let's learn...

A flower in a circle

Numbers

let's learn...

1

One

Numbers

let's learn...

2

Two

Numbers

Let's learn...

3

Three

Your Turn

Write what you want...

 Your Name______________________

My name is Kleyiya.

We just discussed Butterflies.

I will be releasing many books like this one.

We will discover the world together. Yay!

Bye!

Continue

for a

surprise !

Almost there...

KLEYIYA
a musician

From one child's experience to another's experience

KLEYIYA

a book for children

INSPIRED

BY CLÉIA FARGÈRE XININDLU

BY MITTA XININDLU

KLEYIYA

Hello!
my name is
Kleyiya

Today's theme
is 'Musician'

Come along!

1

Hello
friends!

Let's talk
about music
and musicians.

Musician

a musician

is a person who plays a musical instrument or uses their voice to perform, moreso in their profession.

Musician

Mh! How many...?

There are 15 types of Musicians

Musician

Twinkle twinkle little star
How I wonder what you are.

Up above the world so high.

Like a diamond in the sky.

Twinkle, twinkle, little star,

How I wonder what you are!

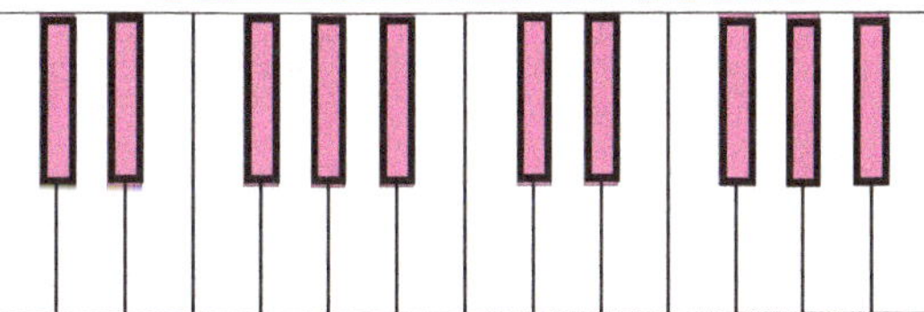

Musician

One, Two, Three, Four, Five.

Once I caught a fish alive.

Six, Seven, Eight, Nine, Ten.

Then I let him go away.

Why did you let him go?

Because he bit my finger so.

Which finger did he bite?

This little finger on my right.

Your turn

Did You Know..?
Music makes people feel much better.
You should try it when you feel sad.

Let's colour

Colour Me In Green and Brown

8

KLENIYA

Let's colour

Let's colour

Let's colour

Colour these drums

Let's colour

Colour these Flutes

Let's colour

Let's colour

Colour this Xylophone

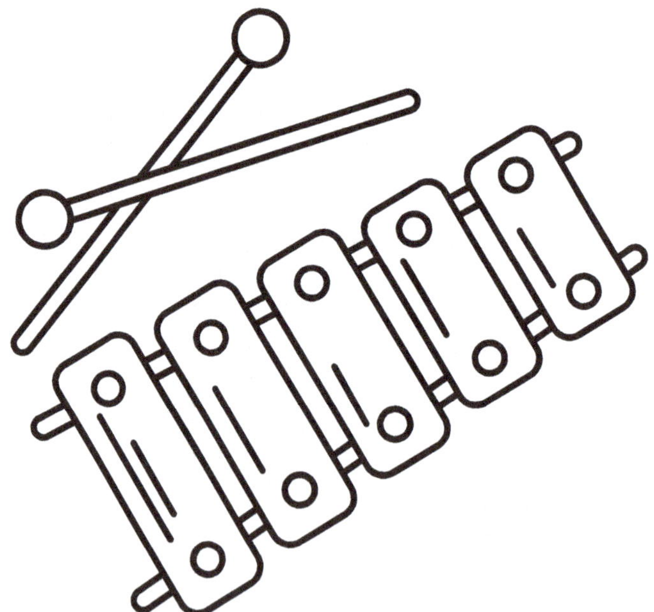

Let's colour

Colour this Marimba

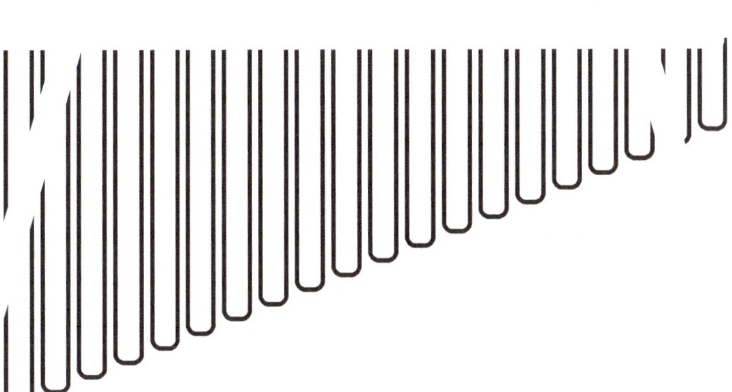

Let's colour

Colour this Ukulele

Let's colour

Colour this Harp

Complete

Complete this Microphone

Did You Know?

The first microphone was patented in 1876

Complete

Complete this Radio

Did You Know?

Guglielmo Marconi invented the radio

Complete

Complete this Piano

Did You Know?

A standard Piano in 2022 has 88 keys

Let's Count

How many...?

=_ _ _ _ _ _ clarinet

Let's Count

How many...?

= _ _ _ _ _ _ saxophones

Let's Count

=______ CDs

Let's Count

=_ _ _ _ _ _ microphones

Let's Count

How many...?

=_ _ _ _ _ _ headphones

Shapes

let's learn...

A phone and earphones in a rectangle

Shapes

Let's learn...

A cello in an octagon

Shapes

Let's learn...

A concertina in a pentagon

Numbers

let's learn...

4

Four

Numbers

Let's learn...

5

Five

Numbers

Let's learn...

6

Six

Your Turn

Write what you want...

Your Name_______________________

My name is Kleyiya.

We just discussed Music!

I will be releasing many books like this one.

We will discover the world together. Yay!

Bye!